Fun Facts

1000 Fun Facts on a Variety of Subjects

Adam Anderson

PUBLISHED BY:
Adam Anderson

Disclaimer

The information contained in this book is for general information purposes only. The information is provided by the authors and while we endeavor to keep the information up to date and correct, we make no representations or warranties of any kind, express or implied, about the completeness, accuracy, reliability, suitability or availability with respect to the book or the information, products, services, or related graphics contained in the book for any purpose. Any reliance you place on such information is therefore strictly at your own risk.

Table of Contents

Science and Medicine

1. Surgeons who play video games are much less likely to make mistakes in surgery than their counterparts who don't.

2. If you get really bored, try to count out loud from one to one billion. It will only take you around thirty-two years.

3. Heroin was actually invented by Bayer, the company that also brings us Aspirin.

4. Every single person in the world has a unique dactylogram. So what is it? It's more commonly known as a fingerprint.

5. Room temperature actually has a standard. It is considered to be exactly 68 degrees Fahrenheit.

6. Pain is not measured in "ouches"; the unit of measurement for pain is actually called dols.

7. The substance that is the slipperiest in the world is Teflon.

8. Don't use anything acidic to clean pearls; pearls will actually dissolve very easily in acid, even vinegar.

9. Going to the doctor might not be as safe as you may think. When doctors went on strike in Los Angeles, the daily amount of deaths dropped by

almost one fifth.

10. Be sure not to tie your tie too tightly. Over-tight ties have been linked to glaucoma.

11. With proper medical care, you have a four out of five chance of survival after being shot. Even more amazing, one out of every three people who are stabbed in the heart survives.

12. The idea of Earth being round is not something from the time of Christopher Columbus. In the third century BC, Greek mathematicians were able to calculate the radius of the Earth with less than a one percent deviation.

13. The one temperature where Fahrenheit and Centigrade are the same is at -40 degrees.

14. About 1,500 people have a surgical tool left inside of them after surgery every year.

15. Natural gas is actually odorless. The smell is added artificially for safety reasons.

16. Tired? Each yawn lasts for around 6-7 seconds.

17. While developing the theory of evolution, Charles Darwin also had a strange hobby; whenever he discovered a new animal, he also cooked and ate it!

18. The pregnancy due date doesn't really matter that much. Only 1 out of every 20 babies is born on their due date.

19. The technical name for human beings is homo sapiens.

20. Smokers beware; smoking is the leading cause of impotence in men.

21. More money is spent on treatment for sexually transmitted diseases in the United States than on any other malady.

22. Male-pattern baldness is genetic. However, men do not get it from their fathers; instead the gene comes from the mother.

Outer Space

23. Due to the lack of gravity, people are actually taller when they are in space.

24. It's commonly known that the first man to walk on the moon was Neil Armstrong. It's less commonly known that the first footstep on the moon was by his left foot.

25. Astronauts are only allowed to eat certain things before and during spaceflight because passing gas not only makes the craft smell bad, but can actually damage the instruments.

26. Even though Jupiter is the biggest planet in the solar system, it has the shortest day. It

completes one rotation just about every 10 hours.

27. While all the other planets of the solar system have an axis that is up and down, Uranus rotates on its side, so one part of the planet never sees the sun.

28. Only 12 human beings have ever set foot on the moon, during the course of six moon landings. No person has visited the moon more than once.

29. The planet Mercury rotates so slowly that one day lasts almost two Mercurial years.

30. The mother of the second man to walk on the moon, Buzz Aldrin, had the maiden last name of Moon.

31. The light you see from the Sun actually left the Sun's surface around 8 minutes and 30 seconds ago.

32. Neptune has not completed a full orbit around the Sun since it was discovered in 1836.

33. For every revolution that Neptune makes around the sun, the Earth rotates 165 times.

34. Amongst the things left on the moon by astronauts: lunar rovers, American flags, and three golf balls.

35. The Hubble Telescope, like most satellites, orbits the Earth once every hour and a half.

36. The time it takes for our solar system to rotate around the Milky Way galaxy is about 250 million years.

37. The largest mountain in the entire solar system is not Mt. Everest, but Olympus Mons, a volcano on Mars.

38. All of the other planets of the solar system could fit inside the planet Jupiter at the same time.

Nature and the Environment

39. There are certain pine cones in North American forests that are so big that they can kill people if they fall on them.

40. There is a giant floating pile of garbage in the Pacific Ocean. Its size varies on the currents and time of year, but at times it can be twice the size of the United States.

41. Contrary to popular belief, lighting commonly strikes the same place twice; because lighting always travels the easiest path.

42. The fibers in a banana are some of the strongest things on Earth. If you were to make paper from them, it would be more than 3000

times stronger than normal paper!

43. There are more than one hundred and fifty corpses of failed mountain climbers frozen in different places on Mt. Everest.

44. Every day, around 50 species of plants, animals, and microbes go extinct.

45. Scientists have actually named the asteroid that is theorized to have made dinosaurs extinct. It's called Chixalub.

46. Saguaro Cacti are some of the longest-living plants on Earth. They don't even begin to grow branches until they are at least 75 years old.

47. Sometimes, after historic volcanic eruptions, the moon has appeared bright blue for months after, due to the dust in the atmosphere.

48. Your home produces more pollution than your car.

49. Every time you brush your teeth, you use around 2 gallons of water.

50. Normal air contains more nitrogen than any other element.

51. In the United States, more than 5 billion gallons of water are flushed down the toilet. Not per year, but every day!

52. Maybe it's good that newspapers are not as popular anymore. It takes around 24 trees to make enough paper to print just one Sunday edition of the New York Times.

53. There is not a single active volcano on the whole continent of Australia.

54. There are around 40 million lightning strikes in the United States every year.

Technology, Inventions, and the Internet

55. Shoelaces actually weren't invented until 1790. Before then, all shoes were slip-ons or fastened with buckles.

56. While most computers these days use megabytes and gigabytes, there is a term for half a byte; it's called a nibble.

57. The computer is not as recent an invention as people may think it is. The first functioning, programmable computer, called the Z1, was built by Konrad Zuse in 1936, in his parents' living room!

58. Nowadays, most people have mobile phones with a SIM card, but what does SIM mean? It stands for Subscriber Identity Module.

59. It is estimated that despite some of the best security in the world, the computer network at the US Pentagon is hacked more than a quarter of a million times a year.

60. The highest amount of money ever paid for an internet domain name was $7.5 million, for the domain Business.com

61. Internet giant Google is a deliberate misspelling of the word googol, which refers to the number 1 with 100 zeroes after it.

62. What is the reason American TVs don't have a channel 1? It is because that frequency is used for two-way radios.

63. E-mail is not a new invention; the first e-mail was sent in 1971.

64. Electronics giant Sony didn't start out that way; Sony was originally a company that sold electric rice cookers.

65. The founders of two of the biggest technology companies of all time, Bill Gates of Microsoft, and Mark Zuckerberg of Facebook, both dropped out of Harvard.

66. The domain suffix .tv doesn't stand for television, but is actually the country code for the island nation of Tuvalu, which makes about $50 million a year from royalties off of it.

67. The man who created the character of Wonder Woman, William Marston, also invented the lie detector test.

68. One of the first working televisions was invented by a man with a truly wonderful name, Filo Farnsworth.

69. Why are pens called biros in England? Because they were invented by Hungarian Ladislo Biro.

70. Washing machines were once run not on electricity, but by dogs running on treadmills!

71. Zeppo Marx, one of the Marx brothers, had a much more successful career as an inventor. He invented an early machine that would detect heart attacks.

72. Heavyweight boxing champion Jack Johnson was not only a great athlete, but an inventor. He invented the household wrench.

73. The paper milk carton was invented after a man dropped a glass bottle of milk and it broke. He got so angry about it; he spent years developing a way to keep milk that wouldn't break when dropped on the floor.

74. Not all light bulbs burn out; there is a light bulb in a fire station in California that has been continuously lit since 1901!

75. Symbolics.com was the first website name ever

registered, having been registered in 1985

76. It makes sense why Thomas Edison invented the light bulb; he was afraid of the dark.

77. Hiram Maxim liked making things dead. He invented both the modern mousetrap, and the machine gun.

Big Projects

78. There is enough material in the Sears Tower in Chicago to build more than 50,000 cars!

79. The Statue of Liberty was a gift from France to the United States. It was dismantled into more than 350 pieces in order to transport it from France to New York.

80. The first and last people to die while working on the construction of the Hoover Dam were father and son.

81. Hoover Dam has enough concrete in it to build a road across the United States, from ocean to ocean.

82. During the construction of the Eiffel Tower, not a single person died.

83. The Titanic actually had a sister ship of the same size, called the Olympic. That ship did turn out to be unsinkable, and sailed the world

for more than 25 years.

84. More than 200 million searches are made on Google every day.

85. Apparently laughter is the best medicine. Laughing reduces the effect of allergic reactions.

86. A little over one third of all the land on Earth is desert.

87. The Nobel Prizes are awarded every year in Sweden, including the illustrious Nobel Peace Prize. Ironically, the person who the prizes are names after, Alfred Nobel, also invented dynamite!

88. Be careful! A lightning bolt can actually get so hot that it can be hotter than the surface of the Sun.

89. We know more about the surface of Mars than we do about the ocean floor here on Earth.

90. It can take more than an hour from the formation of a snowflake for it to hit the Earth's surface.

91. Modern cars generate only around 5% of the pollution that a normal car from the 1960s made.

92. The planet Neptune was discovered through mathematics before anyone ever actually observed it through a telescope.

93. Where does the word modem come from? It stands for modulator/demodulator.

94. Mistletoe does not actually grow as its own plant. It is a parasite that grows on various types of trees. It also has been found to slow the growth of tumors.

95. Think matches came first? Cigarette lighters were actually invented before matches were.

96. The names of the moons of Uranus are named after Shakespearean characters, while all other moons are named after characters from Greek mythology.

97. The cuff that measures blood pressure has an official name, but it's a mouthful: sphygmomanometer. Say that three times fast!

98. Every time you recycle one aluminum soda can, you save enough energy to run a TV for more than 3 hours!

99. In order to create just one raindrop, there needs to be one million cloud droplets present.

100. The sound of the crack of a whip is actually a miniature sonic boom.

101. The electric chair was invented by a dentist, and the guillotine was invented by a doctor.

102. All the planets of our solar system rotate counter-clockwise, with the exception of Venus. Venus is also the only planet with a female name.

103. The periodic table of the elements is seemingly filled with all the letters of the alphabet. But if you look closer, there is no J anywhere on the periodic table.

104. Leonardo Da Vinci not only painted the Mona Lisa, but also invented scissors.

105. The Hubble Space Telescope is extremely powerful. It is so powerful that it can read an American dime from over 200 miles away.

106. It's common to hear on the news about the price of a barrel of oil, but do you know how much a barrel holds? It's 42 gallons.

Miscellaneous

107. Pay attention to what color tie a politician wears when making a speech.   Red ties connote power, while blue ties are associated with compassion.

108. When Santa Claus visits children in Finland, he doesn't ride on his sleigh. Instead he rides from

house to house on a goat.

109. Due to the way computer keyboards are set up, you use your left hand more than your right when typing.

110. When in the UK, you are more likely to find a pub named The Red Lion than one with any other name.

111. Americans don't travel internationally that much. Only 1 out of 5 Americans has ever been issued a passport.

112. Almost all the candles purchased in the world are bought by women- 96 percent!

113. Here's a giveaway; people tend to blink more when they are lying.

114. Your rolling office chair will travel more than 8 miles this year.

115. Almost one of out every ten products purchased in stores will be returned.

116. The Tokyo Zoo actually closes for about two months every year in order to give the animals a vacation.

117. Men are actually cleaner than women. Public toilets have about twice as much bacteria in the ladies' room than in the men's.

118. 1972 was a rough year for the world; that year no one was awarded the Nobel Peace Prize.

119. The United States Constitution, at 4,400 words, is the shortest written constitution of any government in the world.

120. The Pillsbury Dough Boy actually has a name; he goes by the moniker Poppin' Fresh.

121. San Francisco was originally the home of the United Nations in 1945. The decision was made to move the headquarters to New York City because European diplomats felt that San Francisco was too far away to travel to.

122. The most common type of bite that causes serious injury? A bite from another person.

123. Fabric is measured in bolts; a bolt is 120 feet long.

124. More Americans visit Tijuana, Mexico than any other international city.

125. Redheads only make up around 1-2% of the world's population, but in Scotland, 13% of all people are redheads.

126. There are so many hotel rooms in Las Vegas, that if a person were to sleep in a different room every night, it would take them 288 years to sleep in all of them.

127. There will be a Friday the 13th in every month that begins on a Sunday. Also, if there is one in February, there will also be one in March.

128. At one point in the comic book series, Superman had a monkey named Beppo as a pet.

129. Having an office job may actually help you lose weight. You burn about 110 calories every hour while typing.

130. St. Nicholas, otherwise known in modern times as Santa Claus, is the patron saint of unmarried women who don't have dowries.

131. Black Friday, the day after Thanksgiving, is actually not the busiest shopping day of the year. Stores sell the most products the last Saturday before Christmas.

132. In the Czech Republic, there is no Father Christmas or Santa Claus. Instead, children believe that Baby Jesus brings them Christmas gifts.

133. It's actually true when people say that they would continue working, even if they won the lottery. More than half of all lottery winners don't quit their jobs.

134. The name of the flag of the United Kingdom is actually just the Union Flag. It is only called the Union Jack when flown from the jack mast of a ship.

135. The last book of the New Testament is commonly called Revelations, but it is actually named "The Revelation of Saint John the Divine."

136. Opposite to the western world, spilling salt is lucky in Japan, while spiders are considered bringers of luck in Eastern Europe.

137. There is a first for everything, and the first time a cow ever flew in an airplane was in 1930.

138. Once a clown has gained five years of clowning experience, he is then known as a Joey in the clowning community.

139. Rival shoe companies Puma and Adidas used to be one company, owned by German brothers. After one brother insulted the other, they split the company and the companies have been competitors ever since.

140. It takes the average person about one minute to read one page of text. Therefore, it will only take you a little over four hours to read a 250 page book.

141. The number one export of the island nation of Nauru is bird excrement. It's used in chemicals due to the high quantity of nitrates.

142. When you honk the horn on your car, the sound is usually in the F key.

143. Although most people have about 1500 dreams a year, only around half a dozen of those will be nightmares. Sweet dreams!

144. There are always problems with space in Japan. The Japanese even invented square watermelons because they are easier to store!

145. It's impossible to cry in space, because there is no gravity for the tears to flow.

146. Oops! Around the world, twelve babies are given to the wrong parents every day!

147. Being an employee at a fast food restaurant can be dangerous. More of them die on the job every year than police officers.

148. It's always good to show company loyalty; studies show that people who use coffee mugs with their company's logo are more likely to get a promotion than those who don't.

149. The most common profession for the wife of a millionaire isn't model or actress, but actually teacher.

150. Have you ever noticed that in every comic strip, the person on the left is always the first character to speak?

151. Once, in Romania, firefighters could not get close enough to a burning building to use the

hoses on it, so they simply threw snowballs at the burning building instead.

152. An average American child will know the logos to more than 2,000 companies by the time he or she is 6 years old.

153. Whenever a fatal accident occurs at an amusement park, attendance at that amusement park goes up over the next few days. People want to live dangerously!

154. At any moment, there are more than 18 million items for sale on eBay.

155. The overflow drain on a sink has a name, a porcelator.

156. New York taxi drivers together drive more than 1 million miles per day.

157. Every child between the ages of two and eight spends about half an hour a day coloring.

158. Wash your hands, because the average computer keyboard has more bacteria on it than a toilet

159. The record for most known murders by one person is held by Behram, a criminal in India in the 18th to 19th centuries. He is credited with killing 931 people, most by strangulation.

160. While it is supposed to be the day of love, more Valentine's Day cards are received by teachers

from their students than anyone else.

161. Never let anyone say that children can't do anything; popsicles were invented by an 11 year old boy.

162. In advertising, it is traditional for 10:10 to be the time on every clock or watch. No one is sure why.

163. The longest recorded case of the hiccups was 69 years! Wonder how often his friends tried to scare him.

164. Telephone operators are traditionally young females. They tried using teenage boys, but they played too many pranks on the callers.

165. When Mt. Krakatoa exploded in Indonesia in 1883, the explosion was so loud, it could be heard in southern Australia.

166. Always buy shoes in the afternoon; that is the time of day when peoples' feet tend to be biggest.

167. People who die by hanging don't strangle, they actually have their necks broken. Sometimes, for very notorious criminals, the hangman would tie the noose so the neck wouldn't break, and it could take up to 15 minutes for the person to die.

168. Don't shake hands with people after they come

out of the restroom. Only one third of all people wash their hands after using the bathroom.

169. Since 1945, there have been around 2,000 nuclear bombs detonated around the world. Only two of those were used in an actual war, the rest were tests.

170. Most people will eat about 8 spiders in their lifetime, accidentally, of course.

171. Reconsider having an open bar at your wedding; the average American wedding has about 170 guests.

172. Brent Moffett holds the world record for 702 body piercings, ouch!

173. The most popular day to eat ice cream is on Sunday. Or maybe it should be spelled Sundae?

174. The Salvation Army is actually organized like a real army, with uniforms, ranks, and units.

175. Despite the fact that only a handful of people actually live there, the White House has 35 bathrooms.

176. Be careful; more people die in January than in any other month.

177. The most dangerous job in Sweden is that of a reindeer herder.

178. The more formal education a person has, the more likely they are to become an alcoholic.

179. When you go to file something, think about whether you really need it or not. It has been determined that 98% of all filed documents are never used again.

180. If you want to throw something very far, throw it toward the west. The rotation of the Earth will cause it to go a little farther.

181. Every pencil can write about 45,000 words before it wears down all the way, if you don't lose it first.

182. In parts of Africa, be very worried if your doctor does not send you a bill. Doctors there only bill patients they think will survive.

183. A chicken egg was once found to have 9 yolks inside of it! It would have made a great omelet.

184. If you are an average person, you will use 57 sheets of toilet paper today.

185. It's a bad idea to give a dozen roses to a woman in many parts of Eastern Europe. Even-numbered amounts of flowers are only for funerals.

186. Just in the United States, there are more than 2 million millionaires.

187. After ten years, a mattress weighs twice what it did when new, due to all of the things that it has absorbed since then. Use your imagination.

188. American adventurer Richard Halliburton swam the 51 mile Panama Canal in 1924. He was charged a 36 cent toll!

189. Be careful, non-dairy creamer is extremely flammable.

190. If the economy of Wal-Mart were considered to be a country, it would be the 24th biggest economy on the planet.

191. Santa Claus may live at the North Pole, but he actually has his own personal post code in Canada: HOH OHO. Ho ho ho!

192. Every year, more people die in donkey accidents than place crashes. No figures are available for plane crashes caused by donkeys.

193. The Bible is the most shoplifted book in the United States. Thou shalt not steal.

194. Plumbers can't eat too much on Thanksgiving; plumbers do more work the Friday after Thanksgiving than any other day all year.

195. The iconic Mr. Peanut was not created by a marketing company, but instead was born during a mascot contest for children.

196. A Japanese artist once perfectly recreated the Mona Lisa. He didn't use paint however, he used pieces of toast!

197. One of the best ways to get the green out of your hair after swimming in a chlorinated pool is to wash your hair with ketchup!

198. Despite all the conspiracy theories out there, US census information remains secret for 72 years.

199. A driver will honk the horn around 12, 500 times in his or her lifetime.

200. Your birthday is not as special as you think it is; over 9 million other people have the same birthday as you do.

201. Some Native Americans used animal blood as paint because it was almost impossible to get off.

202. Wal-Mart is one of the most successful stores on the planet. Every year, more clothes are sold at Wal-Mart than at all other department stores combined.

203. It may not seem that way, but winter sees the lowest amount of suicides. Most suicides actually take place in springtime.

204. The founder of Avon was a big fan of William Shakespeare, and named the company after the town Shakespeare was born in, Stratford-upon-Avon.

205. Ever wonder what the YKK on a zipper stands for? It is the name of the world's largest maker of zippers: Yoshida Kogyo Kabushibibaisha.

206. If you are stuck in rush hour traffic in London, your average speed will be only 13 kilometers per hour.

207. The country Bhutan issued a stamp once that was an actual record. If you could somehow get it onto a record player, it would play the national anthem!

208. The Crayola color Midnight Blue used to be called Prussian Blue, but since Prussia had not been a country for half a century, people did not understand the name.

209. Janneane Smith once officially married a rock. This happened in Los Angeles, of course.

210. By far, most greeting cards are bought by women. 93% to be exact.

211. Need a new way to get fit? You can burn up to 150 calories an hour banging your head against the wall. Be sure to wear a helmet though!

212. Firehouses have circular stairways instead of straight ones because when the engines were pulled by horses, the horses learned how to

climb the straight stairs.

213. There are only two months in recorded history without a full moon; one was 1865, the other 1999. Both years the month was February.

214. There have been more than 1 million pet rocks sold. Seriously.

215. Due to diplomatic immunity, Saudi Arabian diplomats have nearly 400 unpaid parking tickets in London alone!

216. Except for those in Ireland, all windmills on Earth turn counter-clockwise.

217. Per capita, there are more people in jail in the United States than in any other country.

218. People in Kuwait got so excited when they built the first drive-through McDonald's there that the drive-through line was seven miles long!

219. Every single military in the world salutes with only their right hand.

220. American's don't move that much; more than half of all Americans live within a one hour drive of the place where they were born.

221. Two of the men who portrayed the Marlboro Man have died from lung cancer.

222. Because the American space center is in

Houston, Texas; this state is the only one that allows people to vote from space.

223. In the United States, there are fewer real flamingos than fake lawn flamingos.

224. Statistically, you have a better chance of dying on the way home from buying a lottery ticket than you do of actually winning the lottery.

225. A university student designed the Nike Swoosh logo. She was paid a grand total of $35 for her design.

226. A normal pencil can draw a line more than five miles long before it runs out.

227. Apparently birds hate Tina Turner. Gloucester airport in the UK use Tina Turner music to scare birds away from the runway.

228. In 1915, a phone call from New York to San Francisco cost about $20 for three minutes. That equals $425 in today's money!

229. Most people are familiar with the Warner Bros. film company, but there is another Warner Brothers company that has existed. They made corsets, and invented modern bra sizing.

230. It must be rough on the janitors; the people in the US Pentagon use more than 650 rolls of toilet paper per day.

231. It can be hard to be a man. Men have a 400% higher chance of being struck by lightning than women

232. In many parts of Asia, the normal gift to bring when you are invited to someone's home is a watermelon.

233. By far, the most popular color for toothbrushes is blue.

234. Americans use more toilet paper in the bathroom than people from any other country.

235. Houses that are painted yellow will sell faster than any other color of house.

236. Around 10% of the income of the government of Russia is from the sale of vodka.

Animals

237. There are actually fresh-water sharks, the only ones in the world, are in the waters of Lake Nicaragua in Central America.

238. People are familiar with calling a group of Geese a gaggle, but that is only if they are on the ground. When they are flying, it is called a skein.

239. Koala fingerprints are almost exactly the same type as humans. It is impossible to tell the

difference with the naked eye; special equipment is needed.

240. Chickens can fly, but not very far. The longest recorded flight by a chicken lasted a mere 13 seconds.

241. Roadrunners are some of the toughest birds on the planet; they have been known to kill rattlesnakes.

242. Have an ant problem in your home? Spread some cinnamon where they are coming into the house because, for some reason, ants hate cinnamon.

243. It doesn't matter what they eat or how they feel; horses do not have the ability to vomit.

244. Some of the first Europeans that traveled to Africa were convinced that giraffes were not their own species but a cross between leopards and camels.

245. Mouse sperm is actually bigger than the sperm from an elephant; maybe that's why elephants are scared of mice!

246. There is one stray dog for every eight people in New York City.

247. Although they are all born at one time, it's possible for kittens of the same litter to have

different fathers.

248. A black widow spider cannot kill a rabbit; they are immune to the black widow's venom.

249. While they can only mate with one female at a time, male iguanas actually have two penises.

250. Not only can dogs be used to herd sheep, but it is also possible to train geese to do it as well.

251. Silk from certain types of spiders is as strong as steel cable.

252. Watch carefully if you ever get an ant drunk; they always fall over to the right side.

253. The same as humans, dogs also have two sets of teeth. They lose their puppy teeth and then get a full set of adult teeth later.

254. A chameleon's tongue is about one and a half times its whole body length.

255. The biggest dog ever recorded weighed an incredible 343 pound (155kg)!

256. There are no wild rats in the entire province of Alberta, Canada.

257. Snakes are one of the only animals that are real carnivores. They never eat anything other than other animals.

258. The Lemon Shark is constantly growing new teeth. It grows a whole new set of teeth once every two weeks.

259. While adult humans have only 206 bones, some snakes can have up to 500 bones in their bodies. Almost all of them are vertebrae.

260. The male howler monkey is among the loudest animals on earth. Their cries can be heard clearly over ten miles away.

261. Knees are joints that bend forward; most mammals, including humans, have only two knees. Only the elephant has four knees.

262. We have nothing on the jellyfish; they have been on this planet for more than 650 million years. Even before dinosaurs.

263. A dog's sense of smell is twenty times better than that of a human being's.

264. You've probably never seen one, but one out of every 5,000 lobsters is electric blue.

265. Groundhogs actually correctly predict the length of winter only 28% of the time. That is even less than if someone just guessed!

266. The largest eyes in the world belong to the giant squid; they can be as big as serving trays!

267. Hopefully you don't have termites in your home; they never stop working because they don't sleep.

268. The blind cavefish really is blind, but not when it is born. Their eyes shrivel and fall off as they grow older.

269. Armadillos are actually able to walk when underwater.

270. It's said that cockroaches are the only creatures that would survive a nuclear war, and it could be true; they can live for more than a week without a head!

271. There can be as many as 3.5 million ants in every acre of the Amazon Rainforest. That means that in the rainforest there are more ants in an area the size of a small town than there are people in the whole world!

272. Cows actually have accents; their moos sound different depending on what part of the world they are from.

273. Eagles are one of the only species of birds that actually mates while flying!

274. Relative to its body size, barnacles have the largest penises of any creatures.

275. Giraffes need less sleep than any other animal; they only sleep around 1-2 hours per day.

Imagine what they can get done!

276. Pink Flamingos are not naturally pink; they are a much more boring white. They get their color from the tiny shrimp that they feed on.

277. Mosquitoes aren't color blind; they are twice as attracted to the color blue as the color red. You would think it would be the other way around!

278. Although Polar Bears have cute white fur, their skin is actually black. Also, they are all left-handed.

279. Sharks are the only fish that can blink with both eyes. But you probably don't want to be close enough to see it.

280. Giraffes have extremely long tongues; they are so long that they can actually lick their own ears!

281. Every time a bee goes out to collect pollen, it visits around 75 flowers before returning to its hive.

282. A dragonfly's life lasts only around 24 hours. They had better make it count.

283. Once a female ferret goes into heat, she must have sex or else she will die. Better make sure that happens near some male ferrets!

284. One kind of jellyfish, called the hydra, can actually regenerate its entire body in 2-3 days if

it is cut in half.

285. Most armadillos breed in the summer, but they can actually delay the start of pregnancy until November. That way, the babies won't starve to death in the harsh winter months.

286. Snails don't have to eat anything for up to three years at a time.

287. The fastest land animal is the cheetah. Cheetahs can run as fast as 72 miles per hour (116 kph).

288. Giraffes can't make noises because they don't have any vocal chords.

289. Humans don't have to think about breathing, but dolphins do. If they don't tell themselves to breathe, they will actually forget and drown.

290. Pigs have no idea what stars are because they don't have the ability to look up.

291. When a sea cucumber feels threatened, it expels its internal organs at the enemy as a defense mechanism. Unfortunately, it only works once.

292. There are certain types of ribbon worms which, if they can't find food, will just eat themselves!

293. You may not want an armadillo as a pet, but it's OK if you do; it is possible to housebreak an armadillo.

294. What is the difference between apes and monkeys? Monkeys have tails; apes do not.

295. Leeches don't really seem too smart, but they do have 32 different brains.

296. Sloths are called that for a reason. They are so slow, algae and bacteria actually grow in their fur.

297. Every single zebra has a unique pattern to its stripes.

298. Chickens go to sleep at dusk and wake up at dawn because they can't see in the dark.

299. Scallops can see you coming; they have more than 100 sets of eyes.

300. Lobsters have been found to be able to travel more than 225 miles from where they were born.

301. Only pregnant polar bears will hibernate, the rest of them are active all winter.

302. Lady Bugs are actually a species of beetle.

303. Bananas are a reindeer's favorite food. Maybe you should leave cookies and bananas at Christmas!

304. Each beaver cuts down around 200 trees per year in order to build dams.

305. Americans are dog people; around one out of three homes owns a dog. Only 25% of households own cats.

306. There is almost exactly the same amount of chickens in the world as there are people.

307. Hummingbirds have tiny little feet, but they actually can't walk.

308. People normally think about flamingos as standing around on one leg, but they can actually fly more than 55 km per hour (34 mph)!

309. While being a pig does not sound like the greatest animal to be, they do have one thing going for them: pig orgasms can be up to 30 minutes long!

310. A two-headed snake doesn't really get along with itself. The two heads will actually fight each other over food, even though it goes to the same stomach!

311. When a porcupine is born, its quills are as soft as normal hair.

312. A pregnant goldfish is unfortunately called a twit.

313. Those who love the delicious smell of buttered popcorn should go to the zoo and find the binturong. It has a special gland that makes its

fur smell like buttered popcorn.

314. The female mosquito is the only one that will bite humans.

315. All the hamsters in the United States come from one single litter which was captured in the wilds of Syria in 1930.

316. The adult whooping crane's eyes are colored bright gold, but they are blue at birth.

317. Usually male birds are bigger than the female; however male owls are usually much smaller than female owls of the same species.

318. Stress is bad, even for chickens. Unless they are kept calm, chickens will lose their feathers.

319. Squids propel themselves through the water by ingesting water and then shooting it out of themselves.

320. Turtles don't breathe out of their mouths, they breathe out of their butts instead.

321. Clown fish can actually change genders. If there are not enough female fish around, males will become females in order to mate.

322. Not only do chickens come home to roost, but bats also sleep in a place called a roost.

323. Pumas and leopards can both jump almost 17

feet high!

324. The female lion is the one who hunts, while the males protect the pride and only have to eat once every three days or so.

325. Dragonflies don't seem to need to evolve anymore; they are exactly the same as they were 300 million years ago.

326. Flies can't eat solid food. Instead, they spray vomit onto food to liquefy it, and then suck it up. Don't let flies land on your food!

327. There are a lot of reasons why it would be awesome to be a shark; one reason is that they are immune to cancer.

328. Another reason to be afraid of spiders: some tarantulas can live up to 30 years long.

329. You can't see them, but crabs have tiny hairs covering their bodies that help them sense which way the current is flowing.

330. While dogs can make about 10 different sounds, cats have the ability to make more than 100.

331. More than 30% of the methane gas on planet Earth comes from the flatulence of livestock such as cows and pigs.

332. Cougars, pumas, and mountain lions are all the same animal; they just have different names in

different regions.

333. Due to the fact that their quills are hollow, porcupines will always float in water.

334. Opossums don't pretend to play dead when they are threatened; they actually just faint out of terror.

335. The average heart rate of a hedgehog is 190 beats per minute. But when they hibernate, that drops all the way to only 20 beats per minute.

336. Just like humans, when ants wake up in the morning, they stretch.

337. It is a well-known fallacy that a duck's quack cannot echo. Of course that is not true, they just happen to quack at a frequency that makes the echo very faint.

338. When an octopus is afraid, they change colors from their normal gray to either bright green or blue.

339. The species of brown bear that appears on the state flag of California can no longer be found anywhere in the state.

340. Birds do not have the ability to sweat.

341. Each King Cobra snake has enough venom at any one time to kill 13 fully-grown adults.

342. When a shark is born, it immediately leaves its mother who does not recognize it as its child.

343. Mother sharks will sometimes even eat their babies, thinking they were prey.

344. Gorillas can actually successfully take birth control pills that are designed for humans.

345. A camel with one hump is not actually a camel, but a dromedary. Camels always have two humps.

346. Just like humans, cows also are pregnant for almost exactly nine months.

347. Certain types of wasps will seek out fermenting fruit to feed on, just in order to get drunk!

348. Earthworms actually have 5 hearts. Where do they put them all?

349. With the constant loss and regrowth of teeth, an alligator will have more than three thousand teeth over the course of its life.

350. There are multiple correct plural forms of "octopus" including octopodes.

351. While humans have unique fingerprints, dogs have unique nose prints.

352. A bluebird doesn't know that it is blue; they are

colorblind.

353. For some reason, crocodiles absolutely love the taste of marshmallows.

354. Don't bother giving your cat candy. In addition to candy being bad for cats, they do not even have the ability to taste sweet things.

355. There is a species of fish called the garfish that actually has green bones. Too bad it doesn't glow in the dark. But there are certain fish that actually do.

356. The real reason the Dodo bird went extinct? People killed them for fun because they didn't taste good.

357. Like many birds, owls don't have any teeth.

358. Did you name your pet Max? So did a lot of other people; it's the most common pet name in English.

359. A full one third of all pet owners report that they leave messages on their answering machines for their animals to hear.

360. The only other animal besides humans that can get herpes is the otter

Drink

361. Per capita, people in the Czech Republic consume more beer than any other country.

362. The Mai Tai was invented at Trader Vic's restaurant in California. Its name means "out of this world" in Tahitian.

363. The best wine is actually grown in very bad soil and conditions. It makes the grapes work harder to exist, and gives them more flavor.

364. The popular soft drink 7-Up would probably not be as popular if they had kept the original name: "Bib-Label Lithiated Lemon-Lime Soda",

365. Each single grape vine produces between seven to ten bottles of wine.

366. Pepsi-Cola takes its name from the ingredient pepsin, which was thought to aid digestion in the 19th century, but has been proven since then to do nothing to help the body.

367. Gatorade was named after the University of Florida, where it was created. The school's mascot is the gator, and the drink was to "aid" the school's athletes.

368. While Coca-Cola has been around since 1886, Diet Coke was not invented until almost 100-years later, in 1982.

369. Coca-Cola is actually naturally green, but it is artificially colored brown because who wants to drink green Coke?

370. There are around 49 million bubbles in each bottle of champagne.

371. It may seem counter-intuitive, but most white wines are actually made from red grapes.

372. The Coca-Cola family of drinks actually offers more than just Coca-Cola, Diet Coke, and Sprite. It actually offers more than 300 drinks around the world.

373. The most popular country for people who drink Coca-Cola? Iceland. They drink more Coke per capita than any other nation.

374. A normal person in the UK drinks twenty-three cups of tea for every one cup that an Italian drinks.

375. Good news for those who like beer: moderate drinking has been found to raise IQ levels, and also slightly increase penis size in men.

376. That morning cup of coffee is actually good for you. Caffeine has been confirmed to help with memory. People who drink coffee before a memory test do better than those who don't.

377. Worldwide, 7 million pints of Guinness Stout beer are drunk every day.

378. Surprisingly not Coca-Cola; the oldest soft drink in the United States is actually Dr. Pepper, invented in 1885.

379. Coca-Cola had a hard time at first selling Coke in China. The Chinese characters that sound like Coca-Cola actually translate to "bite the wax tadpole."

380. Budweiser is named after a city in the south of the Czech Republic, which also makes a beer named Budweiser. There have been years of legal disputes over use of the name.

381. A can of Pepsi has 41 grams of sugar. This amount to about seven teaspoons of sugar in every single can.

382. For hundreds of years, people only chewed coffee beans, and then they discovered that they could make a drink from them.

383. Due to the acidity in Coca-Cola, it will dissolve a tooth if you leave it in a bottle of Coke for about a week.

384. In many parts of the world, especially Eastern Europe, Coca-Cola is so highly prized that it is more expensive than beer.

385. Coca-Cola can advertise that it is the most popular drink in space; it has actually been consumed on the Space Shuttle.

386. Gambrinus means "to be full of beer." It is also a popular brand of beer in the Czech Republic.

387. Pabst Blue Ribbon beer was the first beer to come in a six-pack, back in the 1930s.

388. Some Indians in the Amazon will mix alcohol with the cremated ashes of their relatives, and at the funeral, will drink the mixture.

Famous People

389. Harry Houdini was only just a stage name. The real name of the famous magician and escape artist was Ehrich Weiss.

390. What is Ringo Starr's real first name? Richard.

391. Both comedian John Cleese and singer Julio Iglesias are practicing lawyers.

392. Bruce Lee was not only an amazing martial artist, but an accomplished ballroom dancer. He was the Hong Kong Cha-Cha champion in 1958.

393. Pablo Picasso always tried to pay for everything with checks. He found that people would keep them in order to get his autograph, and often he

would get away with getting what he wanted for free!

394. In his time, Michelangelo was more renowned for his poetry than for his artistic abilities.

395. John Lennon really liked women with unusual names. In addition to Yoko Ono, his first girlfriend was named Thelma Pickles.

396. Mel Blanc, the original voice of Bugs Bunny and many of the other Loony Tunes characters naturally has "That's all folks!" written on his tombstone.

397. Mark Twain was born, and also died, while Haley's Comet was visible.

398. When Hunter S. Thompson died, he wanted to be cremated and then have his ashes shot out of a cannon. It is unknown whether this wish was fulfilled.

399. Albert Einstein never drove a car in his entire life.

400. It is possible to have your ashes scattered in space. Amongst those in space: Sci-fi writer Isaac Asimov, and *Star Trek* creator Gene Roddenberry.

401. Elvis Presley is actually distantly related to talk show host Oprah Winfrey.

402. Do you know who Robert Van Winkle is? Sure you do, he is more well-known as Vanilla Ice.

403. Shirley Maclaine and Warren Beatty are actually full siblings.

404. Isaac Newton was not only a scientist, but also an ordained minister and member of the British Parliament.

405. Something you might not know about Marilyn Monroe- an earlier picture of her may prove that she had six toes.

406. Elvis Presley had a twin brother named Jesse, unfortunately he was stillborn.

407. Arthur Conan Doyle is most well-known for inventing Sherlock Holmes, but he wasn't always a writer. Before Sherlock Holmes, he was the first goalkeeper and one of the founders of Portsmouth United Football Club.

408. Mike Nesmith of The Monkees didn't need the money from all the band's hits. He was already rich because his mother, Bette, invented Liquid Paper.

409. No one knows what Albert Einstein's last words were. He spoke them in German, and no one who was there was able to speak German, or could remember what he said afterward.

410. The father of communism, Karl Marx, never lived in a country that would eventually become communist, and never visited Russia in his entire life.

411. Bela Lugosi was most famous for portraying Dracula. One of his last wishes was to be buried in the cape from Dracula; which was carried out by his loved ones.

Film and Television

412. The original actor that played Q in the James Bond films was Desmond Llewellyn. Appearing in 17 movies, he played Q while five different actors played the role of James Bond.

413. You might often see Alan Smithee in the credits of a *movie*. He is not a real person; that is the name directors use when someone does not want their name in the credits.

414. The amount of money used to make the film *Titanic* was more than the cost of actually building a whole new RMS Titanic cruise liner.

415. George Lucas' hero in Star Wars was originally going to be named Dirk Star killer. Luke Skywalker does have a better ring to it.

416. On Scooby-*Doo*, Shaggy is just a nickname. His actual name is the far less cool Norville Roberts.

417. Popeye was, is, and forever shall be 34 years old.

418. Very few people can actually sing them, but the theme song to the original Star Trek actually has lyrics.

419. When Ralph Macchio played the 14-year-old lead character from *The Karate Kid*, he was actually 22 years old.

420. On *Gilligan's Island*, Gilligan is actually his last name, his first name is Willy.

421. Americans love seeing themselves on TV, in fact, 25% of all Americans have at one point been on television.

422. Look closely; the time 4:20 is on every single clock in the film *Pulp Fiction*.

423. Although there are more R-rated films, G-rated films earn far more money than any other rating of movie.

424. It wasn't *The Simpsons*; the first ever cartoon aired during American prime time TV was *The Flintstones*.

425. The lion that appears on the MGM logo is a real lion; his name is Leo, which naturally means lion.

426. The vast majority of the money made on

movies comes from the sale of DVDs and videos, instead of from the people who see the movie in theaters.

427. Shaggy in *Scooby-Doo* is a vegetarian because Casey Kasem, who voiced Shaggy, was a vegetarian and demanded that Shaggy also be one. In the live action movies, he is not.

428. The film *Three Men and a Baby* was directed by Leonard Nimoy, otherwise known as Star Trek's Mr. Spock.

429. Dorothy from *The Wizard of Oz* actually has the last name, Gail. If you look closely, it's written on the mailbox of her home in Kansas.

430. The logo for the Walt Disney Company seems to bear the signature of Walt himself. However, that was made up by marketing companies; his real signature looked entirely different.

431. The *voice* that narrated the Christmas classic *The Grinch who Stole Christmas* was provided by horror actor Boris Karloff.

432. The Vulcan salute from *Star Trek* was created by *Leonard* Nimoy. He modeled it after a Jewish custom that he saw at synagogue as a young boy.

433. The actor who played Corporal Klinger in *M*A*S*H**, Jamie Farr, actually served in the

real Korean War.

434. On the first episode of the TV game show Wheel *of Fortune*, the first letter ever turned around by hostess Vanna White was a "T."

435. The movie *Gandhi* holds the record for the largest cast ever. Over 300,000 people were used as extras.

436. Children's TV legend Mr. Rogers was also an ordained Presbyterian minister.

437. The hit TV show *Friends* might not have been so popular if they had used the original name, "Insomnia Cafe."

438. A character in the Jane Fonda sci-fi film Barbarella was the inspiration for the band name Duran Duran.

439. You might think that everyone knows what Charlie Chaplin looks like, but that is not the case. Charlie Chaplin once lost a Charlie Chaplin look-alike contest!

440. The first person to portray Ronald McDonald was Willard Scott, the well-known TV weatherman and advertiser.

441. Before achieving mass success with *Rocky*, Sylvester Stallone was both a lion cage cleaner and a porn actor. Not at the same time, of course.

442. Millions of people watch the Super Bowl every year, but not necessarily to watch the game. Around 80% just watch for the commercials.

443. In America, there are 5 different possible ratings for movies, the most common being is R, around 55% of all films carry the R rating.

444. The terrifying shower murder scene from *Psycho* is not as bad as it looks; that is because chocolate syrup was used to look like blood.

445. The first toilet ever seen on television was on *"Leave It to Beaver."* Even then, they were only allowed to show the tank.

446. Dustin Hoffman actually came up with the title for the film *Tootsie*. It was the pet name his mother called him as a young boy.

447. Walt Disney wanted to call his new cartoon creation Mortimer Mouse. Luckily, one of his colleagues recommended changing it to Mickey.

Food

448. By far, the most common food item found in homes is ketchup; over 97% of American homes have a bottle of ketchup, more than even have salt.

449. French Fries are not French, or even American. They were actually invented in Belgium.

450. The British really love their baked beans; more baked beans are consumed in the United Kingdom than in the rest of the world combined.

451. Ancient Egyptians felt that eating garlic while performing manual labor would make them stronger and better workers. Studies have shown that it can increase erection size.

452. Honey is the only food item that no matter how long it sits will never go bad.

453. McDonald's serves about 5% of all the potatoes grown in the United States as French fries.

454. The most popular fish eaten in the world is not salmon, but herring.

455. Chinese Gooseberries did not sell very well under their original name. However, after renaming them, grocers found that sales really took off. What are they called now? Kiwi fruits.

456. Look carefully next time you eat an Oreo. There are 24 flowers on each and every one of them.

457. Are you used to seeing Red M&Ms? It hasn't always been that way; between 1976 and 1987, there were no red ones, due to worries about the toxicity of the red dye.

458. Ice cream cones were invented at the 1904 St. Louis World's Fair when an ice cream vendor ran out of cups, and a nearby waffle maker offered to sell him waffles to put the ice cream in.

459. The popular candy bar Snickers is actually named after a horse owned by the owner's family.

460. The world's largest food chain, McDonald's, serves more than 43 million customers each day.

461. It takes 29 cups of milk to make just one pound of regular butter

462. Ketchup moves at a speed of 25 miles a year. That's why it takes so long to get it out of the bottle.

463. Only 1% of all the pumpkins sold in the United States are actually eaten. The rest are used as decorations, especially on Halloween.

464. A cold glass of milk is delicious; but when milk leaves a cow it has a temperature of more than 100 degrees Fahrenheit (37 degrees Centigrade)!

465. Forget the Christmas goose, in the Czech Republic, the traditional Christmas dinner is the freshwater carp.

466. Just one single jar of peanut butter contains around 850 individual peanuts.

467. The reason you see the colors yellow, orange, and red at restaurants? Those colors have been scientifically proven to provoke hunger.

468. Some of the stranger foods that are not considered kosher in the Bible: Camel, Eagle, and Clams.

469. Instead of regular milk, people in Spain eat their breakfast cereal with chocolate milk, or even coffee poured on top!

470. In small doses, it is delicious, but nutmeg is extremely poisonous in very large amounts.

471. They may look absolutely different, but apples are closely related to roses.

472. Just at Thanksgiving alone, Americans eat around 45 million turkeys. Gobble gobble!

473. Pizza is so popular in America that every second Americans eat more than 350 slices of pizza. That's a lot of pepperoni!

474. People in the UK eat one thousand bars of chocolate for every one chocolate bar eaten by the Chinese.

475. Bubble gum is not naturally pink. When it was invented, the inventor only had pink coloring, the color pink became associated with gum, the color stuck.

476. Tomato ketchup was actually sold in the 19th century as a medicine and digestive aid.

477. The inventor of Life Savers eventually sold the patent to his product for a little less than 3 thousand dollars. When he sold it, the only flavor was peppermint.

478. In the UK, for every four potatoes that are eaten, one of them is eaten in the form of chips, or as known in America, French fries.

479. American Airlines found a great way to save $40,000 in 1987. They took out one olive from each of their salads in first class. Those must have been really good olives!

480. When chocolate was first brought from the Americas to Europe, it was only in the form of a drink. It would take more than a hundred years for people to start eating solid chocolate in both Europe and America.

481. When deciding what kind of candy to give out on Halloween, choose Snickers; in a survey of trick-or-treaters, they are the number one candy they like to receive.

482. Corned beef does not actually contain corn. The name came from the fact that it is made using salt crystals roughly the size of pieces of corn.

483. Turkey, ham, and goose have not always been the traditional Christmas dinner; in the past, both swans and peacocks were normal to serve on Christmas Eve.

484. Eggs are rich in vitamins and nutrients. In fact, Vitamin C is the only vitamin not found in eggs, so make sure to drink your orange juice!

485. If you ever see a picture of ice cream, be assured that you are not looking at ice cream. Real ice cream melts under photography lights, so they use lard instead.

486. The British eat more ice cream, per capita, than any other nation in Europe.

487. In a year, the average American eats approximately 18 pounds (8.1 kg) of turkey. That's more than a whole turkey per person!

488. The Chinese didn't invent the fortune cookie; an American named Charlie Jung did.

489. During the middle ages, people thought that walnuts might be able to cure diseases of the brain, just because they have the same shape.

490. It takes more than three hundred pounds of pressure per square inch in order to crack the shell of a single macadamia nut.

491. In the US, almost three quarters of all the raisins eaten are eaten as part of breakfast, and almost all of those are eaten only in breakfast cereal.

492. Until the 1600s, most carrots in the world were purple, not orange.

493. There is more Vitamin C in just eight strawberries than in an entire orange.

494. Twinkies were named after one of their creators saw a billboard in St. Louis, Missouri, advertising Twinkle-Toed Shoes. He liked the name so much that he named the snack cake after it.

495. There may only be the chocolate one now, but the Three Musketeers candy bar originally came in chocolate, vanilla, and strawberry. Three flavors - Three Musketeers.

496. In order to get just one gallon (3.8 liters) of delicious maple syrup, it takes between 30 to 40 gallons (114 liters) of pure maple sap.

497. Originally, Twinkies were filled with banana-flavored filling. However, during World War II bananas were scarce, and they changed it to vanilla cream instead.

498. Salt used to be more desired than gold, due to its ability to keep meat edible for long periods of time.

499. Popeye ate spinach to get strong because it was believed that spinach was a super vegetable. Actually, spinach is no more nutritious than cabbage. Broccoli is closer to a super vegetable.

500. Every second around the world, three jars of peanut butter are sold.

501. You may not ever think about it, but the average strawberry is covered in around two hundred seeds.

502. Eating a banana before going to bed can help you get a good night's sleep better than anything else.

503. In parts of southern Africa, termites are caught and then roasted over a fire. People then eat them just like popcorn. They are not served at movie theaters, though.

504. Don't make a pyramid shaped candy; the triangular shape of a Toblerone bar is copyrighted.

505. The most popular chocolate bar in the UK is not made by a British company. The most

popular is actually Kit Kat.

506. Surprisingly, Denmark, not America, eats the most amount of candy. The Danish eat nearly 30 pounds (13kg) of it per person in a year.

507. In the Middle Ages, Europeans avoided eating tomatoes because they thought they were poisonous.

508. Canada loves donuts. Per capita, there are more donut shops in Canada than in any other country in the world.

History

509. While he is remembered for his famous ride in the American Revolution; at the time Paul Revere was widely known for his job, a master silversmith.

510. Women could not vote in some parts of Switzerland all the way up until 1990.

511. The first person to ever be Time's Man of the Year was Charles Lindbergh, in 1927.

512. The current British royal family has not always been named Windsor. They used to be called the house of Saxe-Coburg, but changed the name during World War I because the name sounded too German.

513. The ancient Greek city of Sparta had around half a million people in 400 BC. However, only 25,000 of them were citizens; all the other people were slaves.

514. More Americans died in the US Civil War than in all other American wars combined.

515. Davy Crockett is much better known as an adventurer, but he was also at one point a United States Congressman.

516. The top mast of the Empire State Building was built in order for zeppelins to be able to dock with it. However, the Hindenburg disaster ended zeppelin flights, and none of them ever docked there.

517. Sailors and pirates wore gold earrings not only in order to look fabulous, but because when they died, their shipmates could use the gold to pay for their funerals.

518. The gunfight at the OK Corral in Tombstone, AZ, did not actually happen at the OK Corral; it took place about a block away.

519. Up until the 19th century, barbers did not just cut hair. They also treated injuries and let blood. That's why barber poles are red and white, the red stands for blood.

520. The first major battle of the US Civil War, Bull

Run, took place on Wilmer McLean's farm in Virginia. Four years later, Robert E. Lee would surrender the Confederate army in the parlor of a house at Appomattox Court House, a house owned by Wilmer McLean!

521. The Pope is not only the head of the Catholic Church. In the 13th century, he was also in charge of setting standards regarding the quality of pasta in Italy.

522. The first person ever born in Antarctica was Emilio Marco Palma, born in 1978.

523. Only two people actually signed the US Declaration of Independence on July 4th 1776. Most people signed on August 2nd, and the last signer, Thomas McKean, didn't sign it until 1781!

524. London has not always been the capital of England, until the 12th century, the seat of government was in a town called Winchester.

525. Queen Elizabeth I of England liked to dress up; she owned more than three thousand dresses and gowns.

526. The shortest war of all time was between England and Zanzibar. After the first shot was fired, it only took England 38 minutes to win the whole war!

527. In 1839, The US state of Maine and the Canadian province of New Brunswick declared war on each other. Luckily, no fighting ever took place.

528. Until World War II, toothpaste came in metal tubes, but war rationing forced them to switch to plastic. People liked it, and they have been plastic ever since.

529. Who was the first King of England? The unfortunately named Egbert, who reigned from 802 to 839 AD.

530. Eight American presidents died in office; four from assassination, and four from illnesses and natural causes.

531. Most people associate VW Beetles with the 60s and happiness, but they didn't start out that way. Adolf Hitler made some of the first sketches of what would become the Volkswagen Beetle.

532. It seems logical that the great Genghis Kahn would have died gloriously in battle. Actually, he died in his sleep after eating too much at a feast.

533. There was more than one reason why soldiers were issued condoms during World War II. They used them as protection to keep their rifles from getting wet.

534. The Aztecs, in addition to ritually sacrificing their children to their gods, were also the first

civilization to require children to go to school.

535. The Hundred Years' War between France and England is actually a misnomer. The war lasted 116 years.

536. The Korean War lasted from 1950-53, and was ended by a cease-fire. Actual peace was never made though, and North and South Korea are still technically at war.

537. One of the weirder taxes of all time was put in place in Russia in 1705. It was a tax on men with beards!

538. In World War II, American soldiers had a nickname for GPs, or General Purpose vehicles. They called them jeeps.

539. During World War I, the tiny nation of Andorra declared war on Germany. They never actually fought each other, but they forgot to make peace as well. Germany and Andorra were technically at war all the way until 1957.

540. Mexican General Santa Anna had his leg amputated in 1836. In remembrance, he held a grand state funeral with thousands of mourners, for his amputated leg.

541. Until 1796, The US state of Tennessee was actually called Franklin.

542. It is now known as the Russian city of Kaliningrad, but it hasn't always been called that. For hundreds of years, Kaliningrad was called Konigsberg, and was the capital of East Prussia, which went on to be one of the founding states of what we now know as Germany

543. The very first bomb dropped on Berlin during World War II only resulted in one death: The elephant in the zoo.

544. When The Soviet Union invaded Finland in World War II, the Finns fought back against the Russian tanks with flaming bottles filled with gasoline. They ironically named the weapon after the Soviet Foreign Minister, and called them Molotov Cocktails.

545. Toilet paper was invented in China in the 14th century, but originally was only to be used by Chinese Emperors.

546. The Roman Emperor Caligula had such little regard for the Roman Senate (and was just a little crazy) that he appointed his favorite horse as a senator.

547. The famous historical lover Casanova had a less than romantic job. He was a librarian.

548. The Enola Gay famously dropped the atomic bomb on Hiroshima, but a different plane dropped the atomic bomb on Nagasaki; its name was Bockscar, named after its pilot.

549. The Hindenburg zeppelin disaster was a huge embarrassment to Nazi Germany, but it could have been even bigger. It was originally supposed to be called The Hitler.

550. London in the summer of 1858 is called the Great Stink. So many people had dumped sewage in the Thames River that the smell was overwhelming; the Parliament even had to be evacuated because of the stench!

551. Fidel Castro was almost a famous baseball player, he was offered a contract to be a pitcher for the New York Giants, but turned it down in order to get into politics.

552. While most Popes are quite old, Pope Benedict IX became pope sometime between his 11th and 17th birthday.

553. It isn't just kids who play in sandboxes, Napoleon Bonaparte would draw up his battle plans in one.

554. Ancient Romans who had crooked noses were considered to be natural born leaders.

555. Napoleon wasn't as short as we think he was. He was actually around 5 and a half feet tall, which was the average height for the time.

556. The military salute comes from the Middle Ages

when knights would raise the visors of their helmets in order to identify themselves to their superiors.

557. Unfortunately, there are no more surviving veterans from World War I, and the last one to die was actually a British woman who served in the nursing corps.

558. The United States got Florida virtually free. Instead of paying Spain for it, they just canceled $5 million in Spanish debt.

559. In ancient China, the secret of making silk was so closely guarded that the penalty for taking silkworms out of the country was death.

560. During the US Civil War, there were actually battles fought in New Mexico, with the Confederate Army riding on camels!

561. During the Second World War, a German U-Boat sunk due to a toilet malfunction.

562. Ohio became a state in 1803, but the United States Congress didn't bother to vote on it until 1953, 150 years later.

563. The British Channel Island of Jersey was the only British soil to be occupied by Germany during World War II.

564. In World War II, there actually was fighting on

American soil. The Japanese occupied a few Aleutian islands off of Alaska.

565. The Arlington National Cemetery in Virginia is on land that was once owned by Confederate General Robert E. Lee.

566. Anthophobia is the fear of roses. The most famous person to suffer from it was Queen Elizabeth I of England. Ironically, the symbol for the House of Tudor, of which she belonged, is a rose.

567. The oldest ally of the United States is Morocco, who recognized the new country in 1776, and offered military aid, including a ship, to the revolution.

568. The United States national anthem, "The Star-Spangled Banner" does not actually contain the name of the country.

569. The practice of issuing rum to sailors in the British Navy was only ended in 1970.

570. Egyptian Pharaohs had beards as a symbol of their power. When sometimes women were in power, they would wear fake beards.

571. The first recorded execution in the American colonies was of a teenager convicted of fornicating with various farm animals, including a turkey.

572. Even the incredible Mississippi River can be stopped. In 1811, an earthquake actually caused the river to stop, and then start to flow backwards!

573. Forks did not become widely used in the United States until after the US Civil War.

574. Pharaoh Ramses II of Egypt fathered more than 156 children. Can you guess where the brand name for the popular Ramses condoms comes from?

575. The reason Saddam Hussein invaded Kuwait in the First Gulf War is because the leader of Kuwait insulted Iraqi women on TV.

576. Oh, how things change. As a gesture of friendship, the city of Detroit gave Saddam Hussein the key to the city in 1980.

577. Instead of normal staircases, clockwise spiral stairs are used in castles so that the defenders of the castle can use their swords in their right arms, while the attackers must rely on the weaker left arm.

578. Wyoming was the first state in the US to give women the right to vote.

579. Until women's suffrage was put in the US Constitution, every state in which women were allowed to vote was west of the Mississippi

River.

Language

580. The opposite of miniscule is majuscule. That is also the proper name for upper-case letter in English.

581. The word "cocktail" comes from a bar which was decorated with the tail feathers of roosters, or cocks. People asking for drinks would ask for "those cock tails."

582. People with college degrees will only use about 1% of the words in the English language in their daily conversations.

583. It is impossible to make an English anagram out of the word "anagram."

584. There is a real mineral out there that is named cummintonite. Don't get it? Try saying it out loud.

585. Some of the first Greek Christians would use the letter X as an abbreviation for Christ in order to avoid persecution. That's where we get the abbreviation Xmas.

586. Maybe you have never heard of a belly man, but that is the name for a professional piano tuner.

587. The word "facetious" is one of the only words

in English that contains all 5 vowels in alphabetical order.

588. There is only one word in English that is pronounced the same when you remove all of the vowels: queue.

589. Not one, but two of our months are names from Roman Emperors. July is named for Julius Caesar, and August for Caesar Augustus.

590. S.O.S does not mean "save our souls" as commonly thought. The sequence was used because it is the easiest to type on a telegraph.

591. One of the less common disorders out there is necrophiliac; it's a person that likes having sex with dead bodies.

592. Carnivores eat meat, herbivores eat plants, but there are also pescatarian: creatures that only eat fish.

593. You could say that whales are the cows of the ocean. Why? Because both a baby whale and baby cow are called a calf.

594. A vexillologist is a very colorful person; he or she is a person that studies flags.

595. The ultimate thing in a list is last, the second to last thing is penultimate, but there is also a word for the third to last thing: the ante-penultimate.

596. No one likes getting fired, but it is not as bad now as it used to be. "Getting fired" originally referred to villagers burning down the home of people they wanted to leave the village.

597. When you dot an i, have you ever stopped to think what that dot is called? It's a tittle.

598. Want to join a claque? It is a group of people hired to applaud at theatrical performances.

599. Hiccups were officially called singultus.

600. Hopefully you never get studied by a Monologist. Monology is the study of stupidity.

601. The longest English word which does not repeat any of the letters is "uncopyrightable."

602. Ha ha! The study of laughter is called gelotology.

603. The shortest grammatically correct sentence in the English language: I am.

604. Subcontinental is the only word in English in which all the vowels appear in reverse alphabetical order.

605. There is an official name for the pound symbol on a phone; it's an octothorpe.

606. You know that feeling when you have a word

on the tip of your tongue, but you just can't remember it? That is called lethologica.

607. The name for the tulip actually comes from a word in Turkish that means turban.

608. The little marks that show the numbers on a die have a name: pips. And the opposite sides of a die always add up to the number seven.

609. Hawaii is the only US state that ends with three consecutive vowels

610. "Screeched" is the longest one syllable word in the English language. Of course, "I" or "a" is the shortest.

611. When you say you will "be there in a jiffy," you probably don't mean it literally. A jiffy is one hundredth of a second.

612. Only one word in English ends in "mt": dreamt.

613. There are nine different ways to pronounce the sequence "ough."

614. Up until the 19th century, it was legal in Britain for a man to beat his wife with anything less thick than his thumb. This also gives us the phrase, "rule of thumb."

615. Maybe the perfect definition for war comes from the word for war in Sanskrit. War in Sanskrit literally translates as "the desire to have

more cows."

616. The word "dollar" comes from an old Czech word "tolar," which was a silver currency used in Central Europe during the Middle Ages.

617. If your name is Mohammed, you happen to have the most common first name in the entire world.

618. There is an actual name for the "You are here" arrow on maps. It's called an ideo locator.

619. If your initials spell out happy words like ACE or FUN, you are more likely to be happy than people who have negative initials like ASS or POO.

620. Professional typists know that "the quick brown fox jumps over the lazy dog" is one of the shortest grammatically correct sentences in English that contains every letter of the alphabet.

621. Halitosis is the official name for bad breath. Brush your teeth daily to avoid it.

622. Have a deathly fear of marshmallows? Then you have althaiophobia.

623. The word sinister comes from the Latin word for left. Romans believed that doing things with your left hand was evil.

624. Next time you see insect feces, you can refer to it by its official name: frass.

625. The sole, heel, tongue, and vamp all describe different parts of a shoe.

626. The word sabotage comes from Dutch workers who threw their wooden shoes, known as sabot, into factory machines to destroy them. They were afraid the machines would take their jobs.

627. Although Klingons don't actually exist, the Bible has actually been translated into Klingon.

628. Jim Henson invented the word "Muppet" as a cross between puppet and marionette.

629. Font size measures the amount of points tall the letters are. One point is one seventy-second of an inch. That makes twelve point font is one fifth of an inch high.

630. The nickname "limey" for a British person comes from the days of sailing ships. The British added lime juice to their water as a way of protecting against scurvy.

631. Don't bother trying; there is no word in English that rhymes with purple.

632. A gelding is the word for a castrated male horse, and a group of them is called a brace.

more cows."

616. The word "dollar" comes from an old Czech word "tolar," which was a silver currency used in Central Europe during the Middle Ages.

617. If your name is Mohammed, you happen to have the most common first name in the entire world.

618. There is an actual name for the "You are here" arrow on maps. It's called an ideo locator.

619. If your initials spell out happy words like ACE or FUN, you are more likely to be happy than people who have negative initials like ASS or POO.

620. Professional typists know that "the quick brown fox jumps over the lazy dog" is one of the shortest grammatically correct sentences in English that contains every letter of the alphabet.

621. Halitosis is the official name for bad breath. Brush your teeth daily to avoid it.

622. Have a deathly fear of marshmallows? Then you have althaiophobia.

623. The word sinister comes from the Latin word for left. Romans believed that doing things with your left hand was evil.

624. Next time you see insect feces, you can refer to it by its official name: frass.

625. The sole, heel, tongue, and vamp all describe different parts of a shoe.

626. The word sabotage comes from Dutch workers who threw their wooden shoes, known as sabot, into factory machines to destroy them. They were afraid the machines would take their jobs.

627. Although Klingons don't actually exist, the Bible has actually been translated into Klingon.

628. Jim Henson invented the word "Muppet" as a cross between puppet and marionette.

629. Font size measures the amount of points tall the letters are. One point is one seventy-second of an inch. That makes twelve point font is one fifth of an inch high.

630. The nickname "limey" for a British person comes from the days of sailing ships. The British added lime juice to their water as a way of protecting against scurvy.

631. Don't bother trying; there is no word in English that rhymes with purple.

632. A gelding is the word for a castrated male horse, and a group of them is called a brace.

have had sex while at work.

652. Enjoy it while it lasts. The male orgasm lasts only about 4 to 5 seconds.

653. The aroma that women find most arousing is that of freshly baked pumpkin pie.

654. The record for most orgasms by a very lucky woman in one hour is 137!

655. Around 6% of all marriage proposals are made over the phone. Not really the most romantic way to do it.

656. It can be good to have sex when you have a headache. Sex releases hormones and chemicals that act as painkillers.

657. Sex is a natural anti-histamine, frequent sex can actually help cure a cold or reduce the effects of allergies.

658. IKEA is so popular in Europe, that 10% of all children are conceived on IKEA beds.

659. Forget their stuck-up image, an international survey found that people in Austria have more oral sex than any other country.

660. Love does seem to exist: 4 out of every 5 married men say they would marry the same woman again. Be careful though because only

40% of women say they would marry the same man if they had the chance.

661. The average amount of time between an engagement and wedding is around nine to ten months.

662. Red roses haven't always been a sign of love; in the 19th century, people used red tulips to express affection.

663. When men are aroused, their testicles increase to about one and half times their normal size

664. Why is rice traditionally thrown at weddings? It is considered a sign of fertility for the new couple.

665. Add a little spice to your marriage on the third anniversary, it's the leather anniversary.

666. Every day, around 230 couples get married in Las Vegas. It is unknown how many are married by Elvis impersonators.

667. Be careful when you answer personal ads; 35% of the people who post ads are already married.

668. Forget the myth of married men being slobs. Married men put on clean underwear twice as often as bachelors.

Money

669. If you flip a penny many times over the course of time, it will come up tails slightly more often because the heads side weighs more.

670. More currencies use the name "dollar" than any other name.

671. You can't escape the taxman. The American Internal Revenue Service even has a system in place to collect taxes in the event of a nuclear war.

672. Despite declaring Independence in 1776, the United States did not create their own currency until 1785. Before that, people still used British money.

673. Bank of America has not always been called that. It started its life as Bank of Italy.

674. 9 out of every 10 US bills contain traces of cocaine. However, the amount is so small that it isn't dangerous, or illegal to possess.

675. While many countries' use different size banknotes, all U.S. bills are the same size: 2.61 inches (6.6cm) wide and 6.14 inches (15.6 cm) long, weighing 1 gram each.

676. In the US, each $1 bill costs about 3 cents to print.

677. The largest denomination banknote in the world is the 100 trillion dollar bill. That doesn't buy as much as you might think; it is in Zimbabwe dollars

678. People have been using money since 9000 BC, but back then they didn't use coins and credit cards; they exchanged cows.

679. The largest amount of money you can have without being able to make change for an American dollar is one dollar and nineteen cents. That equals 3 quarters, 4 dimes, and 4 pennies.

680. There is more Monopoly money in the world than actual American paper money.

681. The reason American bills are green has nothing to do with symbolism; they were printed green because when they first came out, green ink was very cheap and easy to get.

682. In 17th century France, there was a shortage of coins, so people used playing cards as currency.

683. An American penny may look like it is made from copper, but they are actually 98% zinc.

684. If all the gold ever mined in the history of the world was put together, it would equal a cube with each side roughly the length of a tennis court.

685. There are 118 ridges around the edge of US dime. The ridges are there to prevent people from shaving them down. A quarter has one more at119.

686. In US currency, there are exactly 293 different combinations of coins that will equal 1 dollar.

687. Coins in the United States do not have numbers on them; the name of the coin is spelled out in words.

688. The largest denomination US banknote was a $100,000 bill, featuring a portrait of Woodrow Wilson. It was never circulated, and was only used between banks.

689. In Russia, there are more US $100 bills in circulation than in the United States.

Music, Theater, and Art

690. The musical instrument most commonly purchased around the world is not the drums or guitar but the harmonica.

691. Every year, the post office in Verona, Italy, the setting for Romeo and Juliet, receives around 1,000 letters addressed to Juliet.

692. Due to tradition, theaters always have at least one light on, in order to prevent injuries. It is called a "ghost light" and is also believed to

keep bad luck away.

693. The last song performed by The Beatles in concert was one that wasn't even written by them, "Long Tall Sally."

694. The words for the American national anthem "The Star-Spangled Banner" were written during a war against the British, but the tune was taken from a British drinking song.

695. An Argentinean man once left all his money to the local theater on one condition that his skull be used in a performance of "Hamlet."

696. In the theater, it is commonly believed that peacocks, or even just peacock feathers, bring bad luck to the actors.

697. In *relation* to rest of his body, Charlie Brown's head is enormous. If he were a real person, his head would be two feet round while his body only two and a half feet tall.

698. The band ZZ Top is famous for having long *beards*. The only member of the band without a beard is the drummer. His name? Beard.

699. What *if?* Charles Manson actually tried out to be a member of The Monkees.

700. Have an autograph from one of the Beatles? *Unfortunately*, there is only a 6% chance that it is authentic, the rest of them are fakes.

701. Jean Valjean from *Les Miserables* and Sideshow Bob from *The Simpsons* have the same prisoner number: 24601.

702. Millions of people have seen Spencer Eldon naked. Why? He was the baby who appeared on the cover of the Nirvana album "Never mind."

703. The Don McLean song "American Pie" is about the plane crash that killed the singers Buddy Holly, the Big Bopper, and Ritchie Valens. The Roberta Flack song "Killing Me Softly" is about Don McLean.

704. The group Simply Red took their name from their favorite soccer team, Manchester United, who wear red uniforms.

705. Appropriately enough, the first music video to be shown on MTV was the song "Video Killed the Radio Star" by the Buggles.

706. During the Elizabethan era, Thomas Watson was a more important and famous playwright than even Shakespeare. We don't know about him because none of his plays have survived.

707. Don't sing Happy Birthday in public! Happy Birthday is not in the public domain, and still generates around $2 million a year in royalties for its owners.

708. Leonardo Da Vinci seemed to be a modest guy. Nowhere on the Mona Lisa does his signature appear.

709. The name of the band UB40 was taken from the number of an unemployment form in the UK.

710. Violins are more complicated than they seem. Each one is made up of more than 70 different pieces of wood.

711. Beatle Ringo Starr's name means "apple sauce" in Japanese. Naturally, he has appeared in Japanese apple sauce commercials.

712. Legendary funk band Parliament Funkadelic was originally a doo-wop band simply named Parliament.

713. No song is more popular with musicians than "Yesterday," by the Beatles. It has been covered and recorded more than 3000 times!

714. Until his death, Michael Jackson owned the rights to the state anthem of South Carolina.

715. Paul *McCartney's* first name is actually James, and Ringo's real name is Richard. So, all of the Beatles were named after English Kings.

Books and Literature

716. *Green Eggs and Ham* was written on a bet. Dr. Seuss' editor bet him that he couldn't write a book with fewer than 50 different words.

717. We think of it as a common name now, but the name Wendy appeared for the first time in *Peter Pan*.

718. In the original version of "1001 Arabian Nights," Aladdin was not Arab, but Chinese.

719. The first book ever to be written using a typewriter was *Tom Sawyer*, by Mark Twain.

720. The Japanese love their comic books, every year, 20% of all published books in Japan are comics.

721. The biblical book of Esther never has the word God written anywhere in it.

722. Superman, a.k.a. Clark Kent, lives at 1938 Sullivan Place, Metropolis.

Sports

723. Princess Anne, a member of the British royal family, is an accomplished horse rider. She actually competed in the 1976 Olympics.

724. Basketball, along with baseball and American football, is considered one of the only purely

American sports. But it was actually invented by a Canadian.

725. A professional singles tennis match has 2 players, and a whopping 13 officials!

726. The game of Australian Rules Football was invented by cricket players who wanted something to play when the cricket season ended.

727. Some golf balls have been made with the core of the ball made from honey.

728. The days before and after the Major League Baseball All-Star game are the only two days a year when none of the 4 major American pro sports team play games.

729. Johnny Weissmuller is most famous for playing Tarzan in the movies, but before that, he was famous as an Olympic swimmer who won 5 gold medals!

730. The Olympic torch and flame did not come from the Ancient Greek Olympics. Instead they were invented for the 1928 Olympics in Amsterdam.

731. Golf was most likely invented by Scottish shepherds. When they were bored, they would use their staffs to hit rocks at various targets.

732. Modern Olympic gold medals may be called

gold, but they are actually almost entirely made of silver. Guess getting a silver medal isn't as bad anymore!

733. Since the Olympics restarted in 1896, only 5 countries have competed in every Olympic Games. They are Australia, The UK, Switzerland, France, and Greece.

734. Each basketball has 122 bumps, or pebbles, per square inch.

735. The chance of an average golfer making a hole-in-one is about 12,500 to one. And the chance of making two in one round is about 9,220,000 to one. Good luck!

736. Olympics in the first two decades of the twentieth century were a little different than today. For instance, one of the most popular events then was the Tug of War!

737. In dog racing, the mechanical rabbit the dogs chase is scented with anise, the main ingredient in licorice.

738. During the Second World War, there were not enough athletic men to form all the NFL teams, so the Pittsburgh Steelers and the Philadelphia Eagles combined their teams and played as the Pennsylvania Steagles.

739. Badminton is the fastest sport on the planet. A

badminton shuttlecock has been clocked going 332 km/h (202 mph). That's faster than the Eurostar train!

740. Because baseball is one of the only sports where the spectators can keep the ball, an average baseball lasts just 7 pitches.

741. Former football coach and announcer John Madden also spent time as a professional ballroom dancer.

742. Every year at the Wimbledon Tennis Tournament, 42,000 tennis balls are used.

743. The worst sports team of all time is probably the 1899 Cleveland Spiders in Major League Baseball. They lost 134 games and only won 20 the whole season.

744. The record for largest victory in ice hockey goes to Canada, who in 1949 beat poor Denmark 47-0 in the World Championships.

745. Baseball umpires used to sit in rocking chairs during the 19th century,

746. Count them; every baseball has exactly 108 red stitches on it.

747. There are far more professional sports players who are left-handed than the average population.

748. Traditionally, the last event of the Summer Olympic Games is the marathon.

749. Originally, baseball games did not end after 9 innings. Instead, the game ended after one team scored 21 runs to win the game.

750. In addition to all of his other accolades and awards, Pope John Paul II was given the title of Honorary Harlem Globetrotter in 2000.

751. A modern, standard golf ball has exactly 336 dimples. Try to count them!

752. The colors of the Olympic flag; blue, black, red, green, white, and yellow, were chosen because every flag in the world feature at least one of those colors.

753. In the year 1920, Babe Ruth hit more home runs than all other American League teams put together.

754. More home runs are hit in baseball during hot weather than cold.

755. The NFL Super Bowl trophy is made by Tiffany and Co.

756. A Formula One car at top speed is so aerodynamic that it has the ability to drive upside down.

Strange Laws

757. Good news for couples, it takes a minimum of three people for a riot to take place.

758. Bad news for boaters, it is illegal to shoot rabbits while standing on a speedboat in Kansas.

759. In some states in the US, home sellers must, by law, inform prospective buyers if the house is haunted.

760. Men in Saudi Arabia are legally required to serve their wives coffee, otherwise the women can divorce them.

761. There was an actual British law in the 19th century that made it illegal to attempt suicide. The punishment? Death by hanging.

762. In Indonesia, masturbation is strictly forbidden. Anyone caught masturbating in Indonesia can have their head cut off and we're not talking about the lower head.

763. The country of Finland once banned Donald Duck comic books. What's wrong with Donald Duck? He doesn't wear pants!

764. In some countries in the Middle East, it is illegal to eat an animal that you have had sex with.

765. It's always better not to cheat, and nowhere more so than Bangladesh. Children there can go to jail for cheating on exams!

766. The city of South Bend, Indiana, has some pretty harsh laws. Once, a monkey was actually convicted of smoking a cigarette inside the city limits.

767. In ancient Japan, men could divorce their wives if they found out that they were left-handed.

768. In Judaism, it is strictly forbidden to pick one's nose on the Sabbath.

769. Chewing gum is completely illegal in Singapore.

770. It is illegal for a man to wear a skirt in public in Italy. It is fine if it does it at home, though.

771. Cheating on one's wife in ancient Rome could carry the punishment of cutting off a part of the body, but not the part you think. They would cut off the man's nose.

772. It is absolutely forbidden to bring a sheep into the Oxford University library.

773. In the United States, it is illegal to patent any sort of machine that can be used for gambling.

774. In Paraguay, you can still challenge someone to a duel, as long as both of you are registered

blood donors!

775. In Hong Kong, a wife is legally allowed to murder her husband if he cheats on her with another woman.   However, she has to do it with only her bare hands!

776. In a deck of cards, all the Kings have mustaches, except for the King of Hearts, he's smooth.

777. Prostitution is legal in Sienna, Italy, with one exception. You cannot be a prostitute if your name is Mary.

778. In Finland, the fine for a speeding ticket does not depend on how fast you were going, but on how much money you make.

779. In Texas, it is legal to fly the state flag at the same height as the US national flag. It's the only state where that's allowed.

780. It is illegal to practice hypnotism in public schools in the city of San Diego, California.

781. Anyone found detonating a nuclear weapon inside the city limits of Chico, California can face up to a $500 fine or 30 days in jail.

782. In Shanghai, China, all female nurses at hospitals are required to wear red lipstick.

783. In 24 US states, male impotence is legal

grounds for divorce.

The Human Body

784. Humans only have about 20% the amount of DNA that rice does.

785. Check your hair, highly intelligent people have more copper and zinc in their hair than people of average intelligence.

786. Every pound of fat in the human body is equal to about 3,500 calories.

787. Once humans hit the age of 30, they start to slowly shrink.

788. Bone marrow is the fastest growing tissue in the human body.

789. Hair on certain parts of the human body is programmed to stop growing after a certain length. That's why your leg hairs will never be any longer than an inch or so.

790. No one is sure why, but the average American man produces 30% less sperm than men thirty years ago.

791. The human heart is so strong, that it takes only one minute for every single drop of blood to circulate the entire human body.

792. A human hair is one of the most durable things on Earth. They can last almost forever, the only way they can be destroyed is through fire.

793. Being right or left handed does not only matter when writing. It also shows what side of your mouth you are most likely to chew your food with.

794. It is not true that certain parts of the tongue can only taste certain things like sweet or bitter. Actually, every single taste bud in your mouth can taste any flavor.

795. The reason why your shoes smell after a long day? Human feet can produce over a pint of sweat a day!

796. It's impossible to lick your own elbow. When people hear that, 75% of them actually try to do it!

797. The fastest growing fingernail you have is the middle finger, so trim your nails before giving someone the finger!

798. No wonder deodorant is popular; the average adult human has more than 2 million sweat glands, ewww!

799. Almost every single human baby is born with blue eyes; it takes a few days of exposure to light for the eyes to turn their natural color.

800. Over their entire life, a normal human being will produce around 10,000 gallons (37,834 liters) of saliva. That's a lot of spit!

801. Feel special if you have an outer belly-button, only 10% of the population has them.

802. Make sure you brush and floss, because the hardest part of a person's body is their teeth.

803. For people who do not have a sense of smell, apples, potatoes, and onions all taste the same.

804. Fingernails and toenails are actually made out of the same substance as hair.

805. Going to a concert after a big meal is maybe not a good idea. Why? When humans are full, our hearing is not as good as normal.

806. An adult skeleton has 206 bones, but when babies are born, they have 300. Where do they all go? They meld together to form bigger bones like the skull.

807. Almost 25% of the bones in the human body are in the feet, a good reason to wear comfortable shoes!

808. People who tend to have nightmares should sleep in warmer rooms. Scientists have found that people are more likely to have bad dreams

when the room is cold.

809. The white, arc-shaped parts at the bottom of our fingernails have a name; they're called lunula.

810. Strippers earn more money when they're ovulating; somehow customers can sense the enhanced pheromones.

811. Most men hate shaving, and it's easy to see why. The average man will spend almost 130 days shaving over the course of his life.

812. Although it's not recommended, you can have brain surgery without anesthetic because the brain itself cannot feel pain.

813. Identical twins aren't exactly identical, they have different fingerprints.

814. It's not true that blood without oxygen is blue. Veins just look that way because of the way light filters through skin. Blood without oxygen is actually dark red.

815. Soap is made from animal fat; if you are average, your body has enough fat to make around seven bars of soap.

816. In humans the right lung is actually a little bigger than the left one. The left one is smaller because there needs to be room for the heart.

817. The heart is strong enough to shoot blood up to 9 meters, or 27 feet away.

818. While there are many ways to commit suicide, it is impossible to kill yourself by holding your breath. Your brain won't let you.

819. Having an IQ of 100 today is actually smarter than having an IQ of 100 fifty years ago. IQ tests are designed to have 100 as the average, and people are smarter today than in the past.

820. A normal human adult will breathe around 88 pounds (40kg) of oxygen every day.

821. The pattern of your tongue is just as unique as your fingerprint or DNA.

822. When someone is upset, show them the color blue. Blue causes people to release hormones that will calm them down.

823. Redheads have, on average, around 20,000 fewer hairs on their heads than people with other colored hair.

824. Always cover your mouth when you sneeze. Human sneezes have been recorded to travel as fast as 100 miles per hour (161 kph)!

825. There is twice the number of left-handed men than left-handed women.

826. No matter what your mother may have warned you about certain activities, it is impossible to grow hair on the palms of your hands.

827. The aortal artery is the biggest artery in the human body. It is about as wide as a normal garden hose.

828. Your red blood cells have a lifespan of around 120 days. That means you have entirely new blood about 3 times each year.

829. Human beings replace their entire skin around once a month.

830. Most people will spend around 5 years of their lives just eating.

831. Good news for quitting smoking: the body starts to repair itself as fast as 24 hours after quitting, and within 10 years, it is as if you had never smoked at all.

832. After cancer patients go through chemotherapy and begin to regrow their hair the hair may grow back a different color from before.

833. It is possible for a human being to fatally overdose on every vitamin except Vitamin C. So eat as many oranges as you want!

834. Women who snore are at twice the risk of

developing heart disease as women who don't.

835. One in every twenty men has some sort of color-blindness. Only one out of every 200,000 women has the same disorder.

836. If laid out, your skin would measure about 20 square feet (6 square meters).

837. It's OK to laugh a lot, most adults laugh about 15 times a day, while children laugh hundreds of times per day.

838. It's possible to receive a transfusion of coconut water. That is because the liquid in a coconut is almost exactly the same as human blood plasma.

839. When many people eat asparagus, their urine smells quite different. That ability is actually genetic, just like the ability to roll one's tongue.

840. In humans, one of your nostrils is always resting while the other one does the work.

841. A woman in her ninth month of pregnancy has more than a foot and half of extra skin than a non-pregnant woman.

842. 7% of a human's body weight is made up by the blood, but bleeding is probably not a good way to lose weight.

843. Swallowing has nothing to do with gravity; the

food is forced down by your throat muscles. You can even swallow while upside down!

844. Walking downhill is bad for your knees; you put more than three times your body weight on your knee every step.

845. If you add up the length of all the tiny tubes in a human kidney, they would stretch more than 40 miles (64 km).

846. Try to swallow and breathe at the same time, you can't. However, newborn babies can; this allows them to be able to breathe while breastfeeding.

847. The average human stomach can hold around one and a half liters (3.17 pints) of material.

848. 5% of all human beings have an extra rib.

849. People who are on a diet are more likely to have bad breath than those that are not dieting.

850. The human eye is way better than any computer screen. An eye has the ability to distinguish more than 10 million different colors.

851. Testicles hang at slightly different heights so that men don't crush them together when they walk. In most men, the left testicle is lower.

852. Every day while you are awake, your eyes are

closed for around half an hour, just from blinking.

The Most

853. The Monumental Axis in Brazil is the world's widest street. 160 cars can drive on its side by side!

854. The tallest tree in the world is a Redwood tree in California. It is more than 117 meters tall and as wide as a bus!

855. The tree with the longest leaves in the world is the Raffia Palm. Its leaves can be as big as 82 feet long, that's a lot of shade!

856. The deepest lake in the world Lake Baikal, in Siberia, Russia, is also the oldest known lake in the world.

857. The largest chicken egg ever recorded weighed 1 pound (2.2kg)!

858. On average, people from The Netherlands are the tallest people on Earth.

859. The shortest man ever, Gul Muhammed of India, was a mere 1 foot, 10 inches tall.

860. The TauTona Gold Mine in South Africa is the world's deepest mine, boasting a shaft that goes

down more than 3.9 km (2.4 miles).

861. The largest bottle of wine was made by Australian winery Kracher. It holds 490 liters, the same as 640 normal bottles of wine.

862. The biggest swimming pool ever built is in southern Chile; it holds 66 million gallons of water, and it's so big that you can even sail a boat in it.

863. The world's tallest building, the Burj Kahlifa in Dubai, is so big, that you can see it from 95 kilometers away. That's more than the length of two marathons!

864. Over 5000 light years from Earth, the star VY Canis Majoris is the largest star ever found. It is so big that our sun could fit inside it 8 billion times.

865. The Seawise Giant was the largest ship ever built; it was 1504 long, slightly longer than 5 football fields.

866. A woman in Indiana has gotten a lot of use out of her wedding dress. Linda Wolfe has been married a record 23 times!

867. The longest human pregnancy ever recorded was a woman who was pregnant for 17 months and 11 days! That baby must have been huge!

868. The loudest burp ever recorded was around 118

decibels. That's just as loud as a jackhammer!

869. The biggest McDonald's in the entire world is in Beijing, China. Among other amazing things, it boasts 29 cash registers.

870. Minnesota houses the Mall of America, the largest mall in the world. It is so large that you can fit around 24,336 buses inside of it.

The World

871. The only county in the UK to have two separate coastlines is Devon.

872. The flag of the country of Cyprus is the only flag to feature an outline of the country actually on the flag itself.

873. The capital of South Korea, Seoul, simply translates as "capital."

874. Two US states, Maryland and West Virginia, have no natural lakes within their borders.

875. The Canadian province of Newfoundland used to be a separate country from the rest of Canada. Newfoundland asked to become a part of Canada, making it one of the only countries to ever not want to be independent.

876. Maine is the only state in the US which borders only one other state.

877. There are more freshwater lakes in Canada than in every other country on Earth, combined.

878. Seen from space, the brightest place on planet Earth is Las Vegas, Nevada.

879. The flag of Denmark, a white cross on a maroon background, has remained the same since the 13th century, the longest unchanged flag in the world.

880. In South Africa, you can attend the very popular ostrich races, and even gamble on them like horses.

881. Although the area of Tokyo, Japan, accounts for only 4% of the total area of Japan, 25% of all Japanese people live there.

882. There are places in the Chilean Atacama desert where no rain has ever been recorded.

883. Due to the particular way that maps are drawn, Greenland appears enormous. However, in reality, it is only roughly the size of Mexico.

884. The Dead Sea is actually sinking, and will eventually be the lower than the current lowest point, Death Valley, USA.

885. There is a church in the Czech Republic where the chapel is made entirely of human bones, even the chandeliers.

886. In Poland, there is a salt mine where the miners carved all kinds of statues out of the salt. There is even a ballroom and a statue of Pope John Paul II made out of salt!

887. Bolivia is one of the few countries in the world named after a person, the revolutionary Simon Bolivar.

888. There is a town in New Brunswick, Canada, with the very unfortunate name of Dildo.

889. La Paz, the capital of Bolivia, has never had a recorded temperature under 0 degrees centigrade (32 degrees Fahrenheit).

890. The glue used on postage stamps in Israel has been specially designed to be kosher.

891. Going to a sporting event in Greece can take a long time; the national anthem has 158 verses. No one is known to be able to recite them all by heart.

892. The island nation of Nauru does not have a capital city.

893. It's good to be Albanian. Per capita, more people successfully immigrate to the US from Albania than from any other country.

894. People in Iceland just decide not to go to work one out of every three days. Coincidentally, Iceland is also rated as one of the happiest

countries in the world. Hmmmm....

895. The nation of Andorra has no leadership of its own. It is jointly run by the leaders of France and Spain.

896. Despite being landlocked, the country of Bolivia has a navy with more than 4,000 personnel. What exactly do they do all day?

897. Although it has by far the longest coastline in the world, Canada's navy only has about 9,000 men and women in it.

898. People in Denmark must complain about taxes a lot. They pay more than 50% their income in taxes!

899. There are more heliports in Brazil than in any other country on the planet.

900. Despite being so much bigger, there are fewer roads in Canada than there are in Japan.

901. The number of tourists that visit San Marino annually equal almost 20 times the amount of people who actually live there.

902. People love France more than any other country. 11% of all tourists visit France,-must be for the food!

903. Australia is a big place, not including the

offshore coral reefs. The total area of the coral reefs in Australia is bigger than the entire country of Slovakia!

904. Uzbekistan and Liechtenstein are not good for a beach holiday. They are the only two landlocked countries in the world that also border only landlocked countries.

905. Belgians really love their strawberries; there is a museum in Belgium dedicated entirely to the strawberry.

906. Of course there are a lot of people in Asia, but you might not realize that 3.9 billion people live in Asia that's 60% of the world's population!

907. If someone tells you to go to hell, it's not that hard to do. There is an actual town in Norway named Hell. If you don't like that hell, you can always go to Hell, Michigan.

908. Every country in the world which starts with the letter A ends with the letter A, except Afghanistan.

909. After the city of Warsaw, there are more Polish people living in Chicago than in any other city in the world.

910. Originally, Hollywood was founded by a society of teetotalers, and it was forbidden to drink alcohol within the city limits!

911. Finland has the nickname of "Land of 1000 Lakes." It's a bad nickname, though; there are actually around 188,000 lakes in Finland.

912. Jazz musicians used to refer to any city or town as an apple. When you got to the top, you played in New York, hence the nickname, the Big Apple.

913. Got something in your teeth? Go to Maine; it is considered to be the toothpick capital of the world.

914. 10% of all the active volcanoes in the entire world are in Japan.

915. The biggest mountain range in the world is not the Himalayas, but the Mid-Ocean Ridge, which is more than 64,000 km long. Why can't you see it? It's under the Atlantic Ocean.

916. Every continent on Earth, other than Antarctica, has a city called Rome on it.

917. Spain was once one of the mightiest countries on Earth, but you would not know from its name. Spain means "land of the rabbits."

918. There are more cats in the United States, 66 million, than there are people in the United Kingdom, 63 million.

919. Detroit, Michigan can be considered the

bowling capital of the world, there are more bowlers there than anywhere else.

920. The Earth is maybe not as stable as you think; there are more than half a million earthquakes recorded every year.

921. Don't worry about fire in Bolivia. The world's highest capital, La Paz, is so high that there is barely enough oxygen for a fire to start.

922. Currently, 90% of the United States in uninhabited.

923. There is only one city in the entire world located on two continents. Istanbul, Turkey straddles both Europe and Asia.

924. Australia, a country of only 30 million people, issues more than 1 billion postage stamps every year. Imagine how many China must make!

925. The only US state that has a royal palace is Hawaii.

926. The lowest point in the US state of Colorado is still higher than the highest point in all of Pennsylvania.

927. In Marion, Ohio, there is a museum dedicated entirely to popcorn; sounds delicious!

928. Canada is the second largest country on Earth, but its name actually means "big village."

929. In Texas, there is a town actually named Ding Dong. It's not very big though, as of 1990, there were only 22 people living there. Are they called Ding Dongs?

930. The second largest French-speaking city, after Paris, is not actually in France; it's Montreal, Canada.

931. While Canada has 10 provinces and 3 territories, two thirds of all Canadians live in only two provinces: Quebec and Ontario.

932. It seems like it should be London or New York, but the biggest city in terms of area is Davao City in the Philippines.

933. The Eiffel Tower was originally only going to be a temporary structure, but the French decided to allow it to stay standing because of its use as a radio tower.

934. When people were first measuring Mt. Everest, they came up with a height of exactly 29,000 feet. They didn't want to seem like they were guessing, so they just added two more feet to make it 29,002.

935. When you go from the Atlantic Ocean to the Pacific through the Panama Canal, you are actually traveling west to east, not the other way around.

936. It is easy to learn the Japanese national anthem; it is only 4 lines long.

937. In some parts of Albania and Bulgaria, you nod your head for no, and shake your head for yes

938. The city of Colma, in California, was specifically designated as a city for cemeteries. There are currently 750 dead people to every 1 living person there.

939. The Australian coat of arms features the kangaroo and emu. Also, neither of those animals has the ability to walk backward.

940. Next time you have to call someone in Antarctica, make sure you use the correct international calling code, 672.

941. There is a place in Washington called Point Roberts. In order to get there from the rest of Washington, you have to go through Canada, including customs and border patrol.

942. At McMurdo Station in Antarctica, there are enough people there in the summer that there is even an ATM. No idea what currency it dispenses though.

943. Niagara Falls is moving due to erosion. In about 10,000 years, the falls will be around 7 miles farther up river.

944. Scared of earthquakes? Move to North Dakota, there has never been a recorded earthquake there.

945. The Nile River, the longest river on Earth, is so long that if it were in the United States, it would go almost all the way from New York to Los Angeles.

946. The city of Chicago is actually closer to Moscow than it is to Rio de Janeiro.

947. It doesn't exist anymore, but at one time, you could have lived in a town in West Virginia simply named 6.

948. Due to the fact that metal expands and contracts according to the temperature, the Eiffel Tower is six inches shorter in winter than in summer.

949. There is more street crime in Disney World, Florida, than there is in Quebec City, Canada.

950. Tolls on the Panama Canal account for one third of the economy of Panama.

951. The national animal of Canada is not anything majestic, but the humble beaver.

952. The Hollywood sign originally said Hollywoodland, but the "land" part fell down after the sign fell into disrepair in the 50s.

953. The country of Monaco is so small that Central Park in New York City is almost twice the size of Monaco.

954. Who owns the most land in New York City? The Roman Catholic Church.

955. If you don't count the words North or South in the Americas, every single continent ends with the same letter it starts with.

956. If all the people in China lined up single file and started to walk past you, you would never see the end of the line because there are so many of them that they would actually reproduce faster than the speed of walking.

957. The Canadian city of Montreal is actually located on a series of islands.

958. Victoria Falls in Africa is so loud that the falls can be heard more than 40 miles before you can see them.

959. Check a map; Los Angeles is actually east of Reno, Nevada.

Toys and Games

960. The Slinky is not an accident. It was invented by an airplane mechanic who thought that a spring would be a fun toy for his son.

961. Video game maker Atari is so named because in Japanese, Atari means "prepare to be attacked."

962. Monopoly is available in 26 different languages, with the properties changed to reflect cities where those languages are spoken

963. The Monopoly characters actually have names. The poor guy in jail is Jake the Jailbird, and the happy old man is called Rich Uncle Pennybags.

964. Don't worry about inflation; the costs of the properties in standard Monopoly haven't changed since 1935!

965. The name Frisbee comes from pie tins made by the Frisbee Company, which students would throw around as a game. Frisbee is also registered trademark of Wham-Oh; all others must be referred to as flying discs.

966. The video game industry makes far more money worldwide than film and television combined.

967. Make sure you always wear a watch, because Las Vegas casinos never have clocks in them.

968. In a deck of cards, the four kings actually represent four real kings from history. King David is the King of Spades; Charlemagne, the

King of Hearts; Alexander the Great, the King of Clubs; and Julius Caesar, the King of Diamonds.

969. It is estimated that Pac-Man, the most popular video game of all time, has been played by different people more than 10 billion times.

970. Atari's 1983 video game based on E.T. was a disaster for the company; they buried millions of unsold games in an undisclosed location in New Mexico.

971. Stretched out flat, a normal slinky is 87 feet long.

972. The toy company Mattel originally started out making picture frames.

973. Lego originally made ladders and ironing boards.

974. Video game maker Nintendo is much older than you might think. The company was founded in 1889, and originally made playing cards.

975. The longest game of Monopoly ever played lasted 77 days, no idea how much rent was paid during that time.

976. Trivial Pursuit was invented when Scott Abbott and Chris Haney tried to play Scrabble, but didn't have all the tiles so they just invented their own game instead.

977. The reason there are 52 cards in a deck of playing cards? To represent the 52 weeks in a year. The four different suits also stand for the different seasons.

978. The portrait of the King in a deck of cards is based on a portrait of King Charles I of England, who was, unfortunately for him, arrested and beheaded.

979. More dresses are made for Barbie dolls every year than are made for actual human women.

980. Barbie has a full name: Barbara Millicent Roberts.

Transportation

981. It's actually not normal for sinking ships to give priority to women and children before men. That was a specific order from the captain of the *RMS Titanic*, not a general custom of cruise liners.

982. Denver International Airport is one of the largest airports in the world. Its total size makes it bigger than the entire city of Boston.

983. The *RMS Titanic* is the only ocean liner that has ever sunk after hitting an iceberg.

984. The deadliest airplane crash of all time actually happened on the ground. In 1977, two jumbo jets crashed into each other on the runway, killing almost 600 people.

985. Americans spend a larger portion of their income on transportation then they do on food.

986. When the US Interstate Highway system was being built, one mile out of every five was required to be straight. That way planes could land on them in times of war.

987. People have been flying long before the Wright Brothers flew their first plane. The first hot air balloons were invented in 18th century France.

988. Los Angeles traffic is so bad, that every person that lives there spends about 3 and a half days a year sitting in traffic.

989. There is a travel agency that offers nudist flights from the US to Mexico. Once the plane is in the air, you can take off all your clothes and fly naked!

990. Every single day, over 135 million cars travel on the streets and highways of the United States.

991. The Cable Cars of San Francisco have been designated as a US National Monument. They are the only monument that moves.

992. Look up; there are around 61,000 people flying over the United States every hour.

993. The most popular boat name in the world is *Obsession*.

994. One fuel tank on a Boeing 747 has enough fuel in it to drive a car around the world, four times!

995. Everyone thinks about the New York Subway, but the first subway system in the United States was actually in Boston, in 1897.

996. Taxis tend to be yellow because yellow is the easiest color for human being to distinguish when far away.

997. The working nickname for the Boeing 747 was Fat Albert.

998. In Hong Kong, the longest portion of the commute to work is often the time spent waiting for elevators, as there are so many skyscrapers.

999. The distinctive Rolls Royce hood ornament is appropriately called "The Spirit of Ecstasy."

1000. In 1916, a whopping 55% of all the cars in the world were Ford Model Ts.